Shoulder-High

KEYS TO READING

And home we brought you shoulder-high.

A. E. HOUSMAN

Louise Matteoni
Wilson H. Lane
Floyd Sucher
Versie G. Burns

Theodore L. Harris, *Advisory Author*
Harold B. Allen, *Linguistic Consultant*

THE ECONOMY COMPANY   Oklahoma City   Indianapolis   Orange, CA

Design: James Stockton

Cover Illustration: Jon Goodell

Permission to use or adapt copyrighted material appearing in
this book is gratefully acknowledged on pages 223-224, which
are hereby made a part of this copyright page.

ISBN 0-8332-1249-4

THE ECONOMY COMPANY, Educational Publishers
1901 North Walnut   Oklahoma City, Oklahoma 73125

Contents

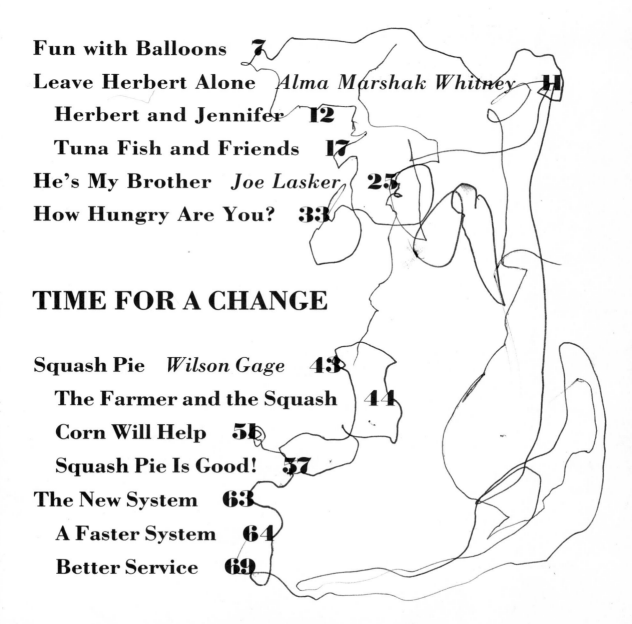

LOOKING OUT, LOOKING IN

TIME FOR A CHANGE

NOW!

A PAT ON THE BACK

LOOK AT ME!

NEW PLACES, NEW FACES

Looking Out,
Looking In

Fun with Balloons _____

We work with words.

blue	tune	flute
funny	puppy	dizzy
soon	afternoon	pool
cannon	ribbon	common

Sound the words.

June

happy

balloons

wagon

One day June went for a walk.

She saw a bird here.

She saw a bird there.

But the birds didn't want to be her friend.

Then June saw Dane.

Dane was a fun and happy person.

At the store all day, she would fill balloons.

At the end of each day, Dane would let June have all the balloons no one wanted.

June would tie them to her wagon.

She would tie one here.

She would tie one there.

Then she would get in her wagon.

It made June happy to see all the balloons.

One day, her wagon began to go up and down.

It went way up.

Then it came down a little.

Then it went way up.

Just then her mom ran out and saw her.

"June, June, come down," said her mom.

"You will get hurt. Come down!"

But, how would she get down?

Then, June saw the birds.

Pop! Pop! Pop!

The birds hit a balloon here.

Then they hit a balloon there.

The wagon came down, down, down.

Now June didn't tie balloons to her
wagon.

But she did tie them here.

And she did tie them there.

They were still fun to look at.

And, sometimes, the birds came by.

But just to look.

Leave Herbert Alone

We work with words.

match	ditch	watch
smiled	used	loved
dress	dry	draw
working	looking	making

Sound the words.

catch

liked

drum

sticking

Herbert

Jennifer

leave

flowers

Herbert and Jennifer

A lot of people would say to
Jennifer, "Leave Herbert alone."

"Leave Herbert alone," said her mom.

"Leave Herbert alone," said her dad.

"Leave Herbert alone," said her
brother.

Herbert was the cat next door.

He was a big cat.

Jennifer liked Herbert.

She wanted to play with him.

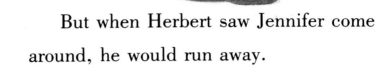

But when Herbert saw Jennifer come
around, he would run away.

He didn't walk away.

He ran like mad!

And that made Jennifer feel bad.

One time Jennifer began to play
on her drum.

She saw Herbert on the walk.

Jennifer was so happy to see him,
she let go of her drum and said,
"Herbert! Herbert!"

Then she began to run to him.

But before she got to him,
Herbert ran like mad.

"Leave Herbert alone," said her dad.

One other time Jennifer saw Herbert
eat leaves on the ground.

She began to run to him.
"Herbert! Herbert!
Am I happy to see you!"

Herbert ran like mad.
He ran into the flowers next
to his home.

Jennifer saw his tail sticking out
of the flowers.

So she began to run after it.
But the tail went, too.

"Oh, Herbert," said Jennifer.

"Leave Herbert alone," said her
brother.

There was the time Jennifer
tried to catch Herbert.

She hid in back of a tree and
waited for him to walk by.

As soon as he did, Jennifer ran
out to catch him.

"Herbert!" said Jennifer.

But Herbert got out of her hands
and ran away like mad.

Her mom saw her.

"You must leave Herbert alone," she
said to Jennifer.

Jennifer sat down.

She did feel bad about Herbert.

She liked him, but he didn't
like her.

What could she do?

smaller   farmer   hunter

closer

sandwich

whispered

purr

He will run away <u>again</u>.

Tuna Fish and Friends

What could Jennifer do?

She liked Herbert, the cat

from next door.

But Herbert ran away when he

saw Jennifer.

One day Jennifer had a tuna fish sandwich.

She saw Herbert walk by.

Jennifer began to get up, but then she sat down.

"He will run away again," she said.

"I could not catch him."

Herbert saw Jennifer.

He got ready to run.

Jennifer looked at Herbert.

She didn't want to be heard by her
mom, or dad, or brother.

"Hi, Herbert," she whispered.

Herbert looked at her.

Jennifer sat still and waited.

"Hi, Herbert," she whispered
again.

Herbert sat down.

Jennifer looked at Herbert.

Herbert looked at Jennifer.

They both sat still.

Herbert was ready to run,
but he didn't.

Jennifer was happy.

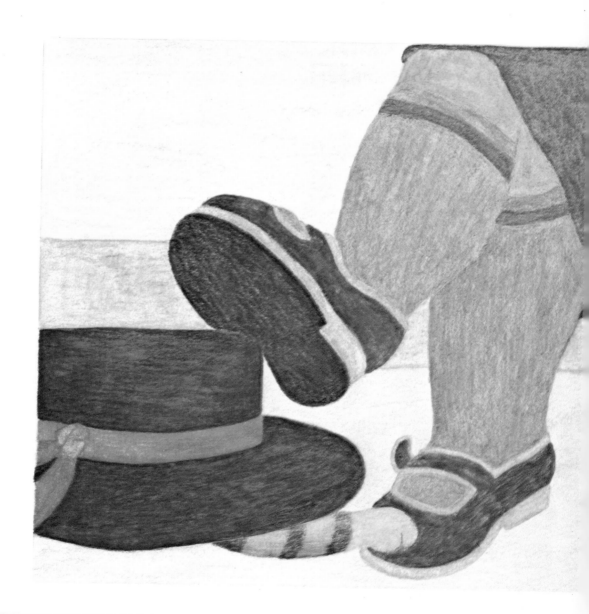

Jennifer still didn't want to be heard.
She whispered, "Herbert, come here."
And she sat still.
Herbert came closer.

Jennifer took some tuna fish from
the sandwich in her hands.
"Here, Herbert," she whispered.
Herbert looked up.

He came a little closer to Jennifer.
He sat down and looked.
He came closer and looked some more.
Still he did not run.

Jennifer didn't want Herbert to run
away again.

She sat still with the tuna fish in
her hands.

And then Herbert came up to Jennifer and
took the tuna fish out of her hands.

Jennifer was so happy!

Then she scratched Herbert in
back of his ear.

Herbert began to purr.

"Purr, purr, purr."

Jennifer scratched him
some more.

"Purr, purr, purr."

Then Herbert got up next to Jennifer
and sat down.

He looked happy.

Jennifer was happy, too.

Her brother came by and began to tell
her, "I told you to leave Herbert alone!"

But he saw that both Herbert and
Jennifer looked happy.

Now no one will have to tell Jennifer
again to leave Herbert alone.

He's My Brother

We work with words.

wrap   write   song

I'll   she'll   you'll

Sound the words.

wrong

he'll

animals

draw

story

Sight words.

Jamie doesn't have a lot of friends.

He laughs.

Jamie is my brother.

He doesn't have a lot of friends.

Small kids play with him.

Sometimes big kids will play with
him when no one is around.

Sometimes kids are mean to Jamie.

He doesn't know what to do then.

School is not hard for me.

But it is hard for Jamie.

When he has to do work at school,
Jamie thinks things are O.K.

But things go wrong for him.

Then he gets mad.

There are things Jamie likes
a lot—like animals.

One day Jamie said, "It would be
good to be friends with all animals."

I would like to think of things
like that!
Sometimes I like the way
Jamie thinks.

Sometimes, things go wrong at school.

Then Jamie gets mad.

He'll run home.

And he'll say, "I don't like school!"

Mom will say, "Oh, Jamie.
You had a bad day."

Then Jamie will go play his drum.

He's good.

All the kids say that.

He'll play and play.

Then he'll feel good again.

Then he laughs.

Jamie likes to draw, too.

He likes to draw trucks.

One time he made a lot of trucks.

They were all the same.

Sometimes Mom will help Jamie
with work from school.

Sometimes Dad will read to Jamie.

Sometimes I make up a story
for Jamie.

It's a story to tell him we
love him.

He laughs.

He's my brother.

How Hungry Are You?

We work with words.

angry	wrinkle	tangle
happier	funnier	tried
windy	cloudy	mushy

Sound the words.

hungry

thirstier

thirsty

bears

hungrier

parts

drank

Sight words.

Their jar weighs six pounds.

It can hold 10 liters of water.

It is bigger than mine.

Does it equal yours in size?

Are all of you hungry?

As hungry as bears?

You would have to be hungrier and thirstier than bears to eat some things.

How about some cheese?

In 1964 some people made a big cheese. It was as big as a truck.

It was about 15,704 kilograms. That is about 34,590 pounds.

How long would it take you to eat their cheese?

Bite by bite, it could take a long time.

So get 500,000 friends to help.

They could each make a sandwich from equal parts of this cheese!

Are you hungrier than that?

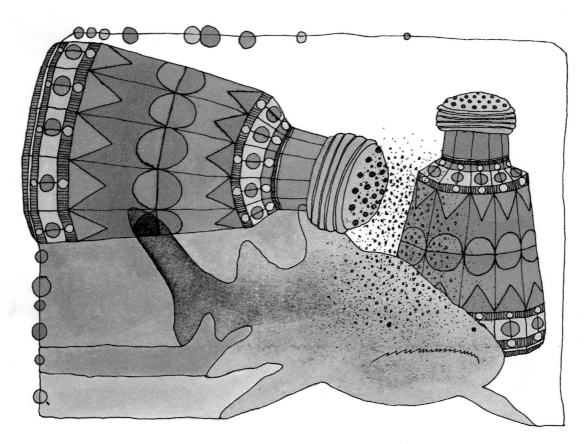

How about some fish?

Some sharks are the biggest fish.

Could you eat one?

It weighs 40,860 kilograms. That is about 90,000 pounds.

It would take a lot of people to equal this fish in pounds.

That is a big fish!

You say a sandwich will do?

A big sandwich was made by a man in 1975.

It was about 678 kilograms. That is about 1,490 pounds.

He had to cook a lot of bread for it!
Some people made a big pie in 1929.

It had 272 kilograms (about 600 pounds) of flour.

But a bigger pie was made in 1976.
Could you eat 5,675 kilograms of pie? That would be 12,500 pounds.

Are you thirsty?

After that food, you would be thirstier.

You use about 6,814 liters of water a day.

That would be about 1,800 gallons.

What? You never *drank* 6,814 liters
of water before?

Well, part of this water will help make
things you use each day.

And part of it will help run your home.

It will help cook your food, too.

Water is good.

You need it.

But if you drank 1,800 gallons you would feel bad!

You don't feel hungry or thirsty now?

You don't like a lot of cheese?

Or fish?

Or a sandwich?

Or pie?

Don't feel bad.

You would have to be as hungry as some big,
big bears to eat these things!

Time for a Change

Squash Pie

We work with words.

squeal   squirrel   squint

eaten   broken   golden

Sound the words.

squash

taken

farmer

grow

someone

Sight words.

I don't have <u>any</u> squash.

<u>Potatoes</u> have <u>eyes</u>.

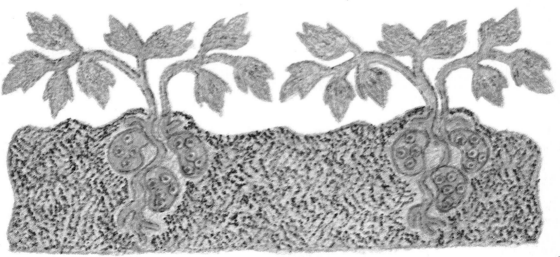

The Farmer and the Squash

One time there was a farmer.

He wanted to plant squash.

He liked squash pie.

He liked squash pie more than
any other pie.

So one day he began to plant.

He planted squash.

He planted other things, too.

The sun came out and the rain fell.

All the things he had planted began
to grow.

"Soon I will pick the squash," the
farmer said.

"Then we will have squash pie."

But the next day the squash were
not there.

In the night someone had taken
them all.

This made the farmer mad.

"Someone has taken all my squash!"
he said.

"How can I have squash pie if
I don't have any squash?"

"That's O.K.," said his wife.
"I'll make some other pie."

"And I'll plant more squash,"
said the farmer.

His wife made a pie and the farmer
went out to plant squash.

He planted potatoes, too.

"What did you plant potatoes for?"
said his wife.

"Potatoes have eyes," said
the farmer.

"The potatoes will look out for
the squash."

The sun came out and the
rain fell.

The squash began to grow.

"Soon I'll pick the squash,"
the farmer told his wife.

"Then we will have squash pie."

The next day the farmer went
to pick his squash.

But they were not there.

In the night someone had taken
them all.

The farmer was so mad!

He took a big stick and hit the ground with it.

He hit the ground hard.

"Someone has taken all the squash!" he said.

"How can I have squash pie if I don't have any squash?"

His wife ran out to see what the noise was all about.

"Didn't the eyes of the potatoes
see something?" she said.

"No," the farmer said.
"It was night and they could not
see."

"It will be O.K.," said his wife.
"I'll make some other good pie."

"That's O.K. for now," said
the farmer.
"But I'll plant more squash."

Corn Will Help

The farmer liked the pie his
wife made.

But it was not squash pie.

"I'll plant more squash,"
said the farmer.

The farmer planted the squash.

He planted a lot of corn, too.

"What did you plant the corn for?"
said his wife.

"Corn has ears," the farmer said.
"The ears will hear at night when
the potatoes can't see.

When someone comes to take the
squash, the corn will hear.

Then I'll catch someone."

Day after day went by.

Soon the squash were ready

to pick.

"Squash pie!" said the farmer.

"Soon I'll pick my squash.

Soon I'll have squash pie."

The next day the farmer began
to leap up and down.

He hit the ground with a big stick.

His wife heard the noise and
ran out.

"What is wrong?" she said.

"My squash!" said the farmer.

"There is not one squash for
squash pie!"

In the night someone had taken
them all.

"Didn't the ears of corn hear
something?" said his wife.

"Yes," the farmer said.
"They must have heard something.
But I didn't think.
Corn can't talk.
The corn can't tell us what
is wrong."

"That's too bad," said his wife.
"I'll have to make some other
good pie."

"I don't want some other pie,"
said the farmer.
"I want squash pie.
I'll plant more squash."

And he did.

We work with words.

three   thread   throw

branches   · dishes   misses

Sound the words.

threw

peaches

dogwood

Squash Pie Is Good!

The farmer put in more squash.

He put in dogwood trees with his
squash, too.

"Why did you plant all these dogwood trees?" said his wife.

"Dogwood trees have a bark," said the farmer.
"The potatoes can see someone.
When they do, the dogwood trees can bark.
That will tell us.
The ears of corn can hear someone.
When they do, the dogwood trees can bark.
That will tell us.
This time no one will take the squash."

The squash got bigger and bigger.

"Soon we will have squash pie," said the farmer.

The next day he went out to pick
the squash.

But the squash were not there.

In the night someone had taken
them all.

The eyes of the potatoes did
not see.

The ears of the corn did not hear.

So the dogwood trees did not bark.

"No squash," said the farmer.

"There, there," said his wife.
"You will have squash pie."

She got some big peaches.
She threw them into the air.
She threw more peaches into the air.
The peaches came down—SQUASH!
She took the peaches in.
Then she made a squash pie.

"Oh, this pie is good," said
the farmer.

"It is," said his wife.
"I was wrong all the time.
I didn't think squash pie would
be good.
But this pie is good!"

The New System

We work with words.

berry   tomorrow   carry

spray   spring   spread

valley   honey   turkey

girl's   king's   cat's

Sound the words.

sorry

sprinkler

money

porch

Bennett's

Sight words.

<u>Gladys</u> heard from <u>Ms.</u> Bennett.

It's my new <u>system</u>.

A Faster System

Gladys went down the street.

She took out a paper and threw
it onto a porch.

She went faster.

At the next home she threw a paper
onto the porch.

Next she threw a paper at Ms.
Bennett's porch.

It fell into the flowers.

But Gladys didn't stop.
"Oh, well, she will see it,"
said Gladys.

Gladys wanted to do her work faster
than she ever had before.

It was her new system.

If she did her work faster, she could
collect her money faster.

When she got home, she heard
from Ms. Bennett.

"Gladys, do you have a paper
for me?"

"Oh, yes," Gladys said.
"I threw it at the porch.
I think it went into the flowers."

"Oh, Gladys!" said Ms. Bennett.
"We don't know where to look
for the paper.
One time it was under the porch.
One time it was up in the tree.
Now it's in the flowers."

"I'm sorry," said Gladys.
"But it's my new system."

The next day, too, Gladys threw
each paper as she went by.

When she came to Ms. Bennett's home,
she threw the paper hard at the porch.

The paper didn't hit the porch.

It went under the sprinkler.

Gladys was sorry the paper went under
the sprinkler.

But she didn't stop.

She didn't think she had time.

She wanted to do her work faster than
she ever had before.

This was the day to collect her money.

test   fast   stalks   rest

Do you know what good <u>service</u> is?

Gladys went to a <u>lot</u> of <u>trouble</u>.

Better Service

Gladys had made it home in time to go out and collect her money.

She came to collect at the Bennett's home before all the rest.

Ms. Bennett's paper was still under the sprinkler.

But Ms. Bennett looked happy when
she came to the door.

"I have the money ready," she said.
"I put it where I had to look for
each paper.
Have fun, Gladys."

Ms. Bennett went into her home.

Gladys looked around.
She saw the paper under the sprinkler.
Next to it was some money.

She ran under the sprinkler and
got the paper and the money.
Then she ran back to the porch.
Gladys was not happy.

That was some of the money.

But where was the rest of it?

Gladys looked around some more.

She looked way up in the branches of the tree.

There was more money.

Gladys went up, up, up the tree.

She had a lot of trouble.

And still she had to look for some more of the money.

"Is there some other place to
look?" Gladys said.

"Oh, yes.
Under the porch!"

Gladys had to crawl under the porch.

There she saw more money.

But still there had to be a little
more.

Gladys sat down to think.

Where was the rest?

"The flowers!" she said.

"The other day the paper went
into the flowers."

Gladys had to crawl into them
to get the rest of the money.

When she tried to back out,
she scratched her hands.

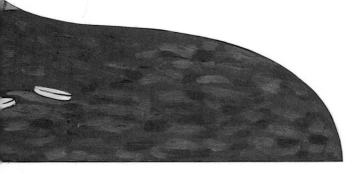

Now she had all the money.

But how hard she had to work to
get it!

She sat down to think.

Was this what people did to get
each paper she threw?

Was this good service?

Gladys went over and got a new
paper.

She went to Ms. Bennett's
door.

"Ms. Bennett," she said, "I have
something new in my system.

I call it service.

Do you know what service means?

I do.

It means you will see the paper
on the porch each day."

Now!

Oh No, Cat!_____

We work with words.

place   city   cent

fence   dance

Sound the words.

nice

chance

we'll

family

Sight words.

"Give me the <u>chair</u>," said <u>father</u>.

I can play the <u>piano</u>.

The cat said, "<u>Meow!</u>"

At the door one day the father
saw a cat.

There was a note on the cat.
"Keep this cat," the note said.
"It must have a home."

"What will we do with it?" said
the father.

"We'll keep it," said the family.
"It must have a home.
It's a good cat."

"Meow?" said the cat.
"Meow? Meow?"

The cat got up on the chair.
It hit the flowers.

"Look!" said the father. "What
will we do with it?"

"We'll keep it," said the family.
"Give it one more chance."

The cat began to crawl up
the chair.

The father was mad.
The mother said, "It's a good cat.
It has a purr that's so nice."

"Give it one more chance," said
the family.

The cat tried to make friends
with people.

It would hide in back of the door.

When people went by, it would leap
on them.

This made the father mad.

Some people didn't want to
be friends.

"It's fun to play with," said
the girl.

"Give it one more chance," said
the family.

The cat would walk across the floor
and make tracks.

This made the father so mad!

"What will we do with it?"
said the father.

"It's fun to look at,"
said the boy.

"Give it one more chance,"
said the family.

In the night the cat began to walk
on the piano.

The family heard the noise and got up.

"What are we going to do with this
cat?" said the father.

"Give it one more chance," said
the mother.

"It's so nice," said the girl.

"It will be good," said the boy.

"It will?" said the father.

The father looked down at the cat
on the piano.

The cat began to purr.

"It is nice," said the father.

"Do you think it will be good?"

"Oh, yes," said the family.

"Then we'll keep it," the father said.

"We'll give it one more chance."

A Place to Live _____

We work with words.

swam   sweet   sway

Sound the words.

swift

house

frogs

cave

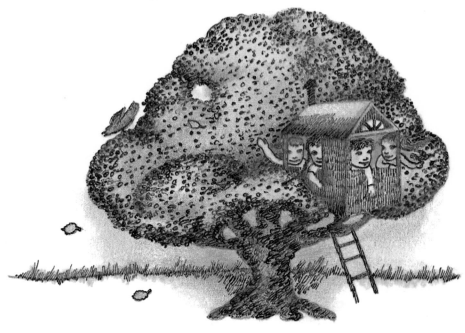

Why don't people live in trees?

Birds live in trees.

Other animals live there, too.

So, why not people up in the red leaves?

Things fall out of trees.

A swift wind comes and down comes

the piano.

Down comes the bed.

Down comes the chair.

And down come the people.

Trees make good houses, but just for the birds.

What about a house on the water?

The fish and frogs live there.
The turtle lives there, too.
So why not people out on the waves?

A house will go under if it gets a
hole in the floor.
Then the people must swim back to
the land.
Leave the water to the frogs.

What about a home in a cave?

People a long time back made their
home in a cave.
But now the bears live there.

Bears can get mad over just a
little thing.

Bears don't want people in their cave.
It's better to let the bears have the
cave.

So where is the best house for
people?

It's not in a tree.
It's not on the waves.
And it's not in a cave.

Maybe the best place is just where
we are.

The King's Wish

We work with words.

spear   space   Spain

chill   choose   chimney

Sound the words.

spots

children

test

king's

open

sick

Sight word.

<u>Christine</u> is happy.

The king of Quig was a good king.

All day, each day, he would ride
around Quig.

He had to see that everyone was
well and happy.

One day the king saw a man with
some fish.

The king said, "Oh, it must be fun
to fish!

How I wish I had time to fish."

The three children of the king heard
his wish.

That night they went to see the king.

Christine said, "Father, we heard
your wish.

We want you to have time to go
and fish.

We'll do your work for you."

The king said, "Why, you are
just children!

But maybe you could do my work.

Let's see.

I will give you a test—a
king's test."

Then he said, "I will take you
to the king's test room."

Now the three children were in the king's test room.

They looked all around.

The king said to them, "I will shut this door.

You must not open it.

But you must get out of the room.

Can you do it?"

The children saw just one door.

But the king had said they could not

open it.

They would have to get out some

other way.

"Look," said Christine.

"Maybe we can get out that window."

They tried the window but they

were all too big.

Don and Christine looked way down
next to the floor.

All they saw there was a small
hole.

Jill said, "Look!

Here is some red ink.

Maybe we can get out with this.

Let's put red spots all over us

with this ink."

"Yes," said Don, "let's do.

The king's man will look into

this room.

He'll see us and think we

are sick."

Soon the king's man did look

into the king's test room.

"Open that door!" the king's man said.

"The king's children are sick.

Get the king!"

The children had red spots all
over them.

The man went in and took the
children out the door.

The king saw that his children
were out of the room.

He saw that the spots were red ink.

He saw that they were not sick.

"You did it!" he said.

"You got out of the room and you
didn't open the door.

My man did!"

Then the king said, "You are
just children.

But you can do a king's work."

The king said good-by to his
children and he went to fish.

Mr. Spats

Shel Silverstein

Mr. Spats
had twenty-six hats
and none of them was the same.
And Mr. Smeds
had twenty-six heads
and only one hat to his name.

Now when Mr. Smeds
met Mr. Spats,
they talked about
buying hats. . . .

And Mr. Spats
bought Mr. Smed's hat!
Did you ever hear
of anything
crazier
than
that?

A Pat on the Back

Natsook

We work with words.

could   would   tour

saved   named   waded

soft   moss   off

Sound the words.

should

Natsook

smiled

watched

songs

tonight

Sight words.

<u>Kitapko</u> took a fish from the water.

Don't get <u>discouraged</u>.

103

Natsook and Kitapko

"I wish I could fish as well
as you," said Natsook.

Kitapko smiled.
"It will take a lot of time.
There is a lot to know," he
said.

"Help me," said Natsook.

"I should like to know the things
you know."

"Well, it's not as hard if you
put the line in the water."

Now Natsook smiled.
His line was out of the water
and was next to him on the ice.
He watched Kitapko too much.

"But when my line is in the
water, the fish don't tug on it.
I get discouraged," said Natsook.

"It's hard," said Kitapko.
"But don't get discouraged."

Kitapko took a fish from
the hole in the ice.
He put it on his big pile of
fish.

Then Natsook began to fish.
He sat on the ice just as Kitapko
did.
He let the line down.
He took the line up.
He did all the things that
Kitapko did.
But the fish didn't tug on his line.

"Should I sing?" said Natsook.

"Will that help?"

"Yes, that should help," said Kitapko.

"When I fish, I like to sing."

"What songs do you sing?"
Natsook said.

"My songs would not help you,"
Kitapko said, and he smiled.

"You must feel songs deep down.

If you don't, they won't work.

The fish will know."

Natsook began to feel discouraged.

"But I can't sing.

And I know I can't fish.

I think I'll just go home."

"Here, take these," said Kitapko.

Natsook took the fish from Kitapko.

"You are too good to me,"
said Natsook.
"Tonight we'll eat fish.
Tonight no one will be hungry."

Natsook took the fish home
with him.

He didn't think he wanted to
fish ever again.

price   prince   present   pride

farmers   painters   speakers   hunters

won

Only hunters could have a wolverine tail.

Natsook was in trouble.

Natsook and the Wolverine Tail

Natsook went down the road to his home.

His mother saw him come.

She said to everyone, "Look at all the fish Natsook took from the sea.

Soon he'll be one of the hunters."

"I was with Kitapko," said Natsook.

"These fish are his."

Everyone was so happy for Natsook

that they made a lot of noise.

So no one heard what he said.

The noise went down when Natsook's father came.

Natsook began to say, "I was with Kitapko.
He had a big pile of fish so he . . ."

But Natsook had to stop when he looked at his father.

There was pride in the eyes of Natsook's father.

His father said with pride,"Soon
you will be one of the hunters.
I want you to put this on."

His father took his wolverine
tail and put it in Natsook's hands.

A wolverine tail was for hunters.
But Natsook said nothing.

Soon the sun was up.

Natsook went out on the ice.

He had to talk with Kitapko.

But Kitapko was not there.

So Natsook let his line down
into the water.

He began to fish.

It was good to be out alone.

Natsook began to feel happy.

He began to sing.

Soon there was a tug on the line.

Then there was one more tug.

Natsook took fish after fish out of
the water.

Soon he had a big pile of fish.

"Natsook!"

It was Kitapko.

He saw Natsook's pile of fish.

"Did you catch all these fish?" he said.

"Yes, I did, " said Natsook.

"But, Kitapko, I am in trouble.

Big trouble! "

Then Natsook told Kitapko about the
night before.

"What can I do?" he said.

Kitapko smiled.

"Only a boy that can catch fish like
this gets the wolverine tail.

Your family should take pride in you."

"But I got the wolverine tail last
night!"

"Yes, but you have won it now,"
said Kitapko.

"Yes, you have won it.

Now you can be one of the hunters."

No Cows Where Morris Lived

We work with words.

fixture	pasture	furniture
bows	pies	plays
brave	brick	brace

Sound the words.

picture

cows

brown

moo

Sight word.

No one would <u>believe</u> Morris.

Morris never saw cows.

There were no cows in the house
where Morris lived.

No cows went down the streets.

There were no cows that rode
the buses.

No cows came to eat the grass
by his home.

There were no cows at all!

Morris saw a picture of some
cows.

But a picture is just a picture.

With a picture you could not
feel the brown hide of a cow.

And you could not hear a cow moo.

Morris had wanted to see a
cow from the time he was small.

But he never had.

And now he was in grade school!

One day on his way to school, Morris
began to think about cows.

"Oh, I wish I could see a cow,"
Morris said.

He went on down the street and came
face to face with. . .a cow!

Could Morris believe his eyes?

"Oh!" said Morris.

"Can this be?"

He shut his eyes for a time.

Then he looked again.

But the cow didn't go away.

Morris looked at the cow.

The cow looked back at Morris.

It was a brown cow with a rope
around its neck.

It had nice brown eyes.

Morris smiled.

"Have you come to be with
me?" Morris said to the cow.

He picked up the rope that was
around its neck.

The cow began to moo.

What a nice noise!

Then it went with Morris down
the street.

Everyone began to stop and look.

A girl said to her mother, "Is
that a cow?"

A man said, "My, that's a
big dog!

It's way too big for a small boy!"

A boy rode by on his bike.

When he saw the cow, he rode
over a hole!

Morris took his cow on down the
street.

When they came to the school,
Morris let go of the rope.

"You stay here," he told the
cow.

"I have to go to school."

In school, no one would believe
that Morris had a cow.

So some of the children went out
to see.

The cow began to moo.

Soon everyone went out to look
at the cow.

A big truck with two people in it
came down the street.

"There she is!" said the man.

The truck came to a stop.
The man got out.
He picked up the rope and took
the cow to the back of the truck.
Other cows were there, too.
They all began to moo.

"Where will you take my cow?"
said Morris.

"We'll take her and these other cows
to a new farm," said the man.

"This cow got off the truck when
we had to stop.

I can't think why she did that!"

Morris smiled.

He began to think about his
wish.

He could think why the cow got
off the truck.

The truck moved away.

The cow looked back at Morris

with her big brown eyes.

Morris saw that the cow smiled.

Max

We work with words.

cries   dries   skies

Sundays   Mondays

prance   since   chance

Sound the words.

goes

Saturdays

dance

class

Sight words.

Max <u>says</u> "O.K.

But first, I must put on my <u>shoes</u>."

His sister, <u>Lisa</u>, can dance.

Max can play ball well.

He can run and leap.

And he can catch any ball.

On Saturdays he goes to the park.

There he can play with his team.

One Saturday he goes with his
sister Lisa to her dance class.

Her school is on the way
to the park.

Soon Max and Lisa get to the school.

Max still has a lot of time before
he must be at the park.

His sister asks him if he would like
to come in for a time.

Max doesn't want to, but . . .

"O.K.," he says.

Soon the class will begin.

Max goes over to get a chair.

He wants to sit by the door.

From there he can see
the class dance.

When it's time, he'll leave to go
to the park.

He must have time to get ready
to play ball.

The teacher asks Max to dance
with the class.

Max says he will.

But he must take off his
shoes first.

Max does what the class does.

"This is fun," says Max.

The class is ready to do a
leap.

But it's time for Max to leave.

Max doesn't want to go before he can leap.

So he does that first.

He gets his shoes as he must leave.

Leap, leap, leap, all the way
to the park.

He's not on time.

But everyone has waited for him.

He goes up to bat.

Strike one!

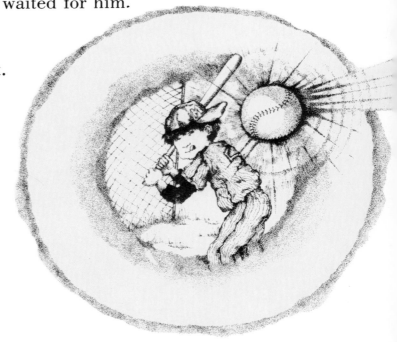

He tries one more time.

Strike two!

And then. . .

A home run!

Now Max has a new way to get ready
to play ball on Saturdays.

He goes to dance class.

Look at Me!

Alfred Snood

We work with words.

Fred   front   refreshing

waited   landed   hated

Sound the words.

Alfred

Snood

painted

Alfred Snood is my friend.

But no one can see him but me.

The other day someone put snow
in here.

Alfred Snood did it.

I think he was the one that hit
my little brother, too.

He tries to be good.

But Alfred Snood is small and
sometimes he just can't be good.

One day my mother painted the house.

Then she had to leave to talk to

a friend.

Alfred Snood got into her things.

By the time she came back, he

had painted a lot of things.

He had painted the cat.

He had painted a door.

And the kids next door.

And the Bennetts' truck.

Then Alfred Snood ran, and someone
said I did it.

But he's not all bad.
He tries to be nice.

He never asks people why
they are so big.
He's good to small animals
a lot of the time.
He won't take ants into the
house.
And Alfred Snood likes to take
a bath.

But not a lot.

When it's time for bed, he will make
only a little noise.

Alfred Snood is my friend, and
no one can see him but me.

Going to Bed

Marchette Chute

I'm always told to hurry up—
Which I'd be glad to do,
If there were not so many things
That need attending to.

But first I have to find my towel
Which fell behind the rack,
And when a pillow's thrown at me
I have to throw it back.

And then I have to get the things
I need in bed with me.
Like marbles and my birthday train
And Pete the chimpanzee.

I have to see my polliwog
Is safely in its pan,
And stand a minute on my head
To be quite sure I can.

I have to bounce upon my bed
To see if it will sink,
And then when I am covered up
I find I need a drink.

Mushy Eggs

We work with words.

June	Janet	Jimmy
rusty	bossy	rainy
spill	speak	spank

Sound the words.

Jane

mushy

eggs

Spain

while

Molly

Sight words.

Jane <u>cares</u> for us.

Mushy eggs are like <u>scrambled</u> eggs.

I am Will, and this is my
brother Sam.

We live in a house with my mom.

She goes to work where they have
a computer.

One time she let us go with her.

We watched her work on the computer.

This is the house where Dad
lives.

He doesn't live with us.

Dad can draw and paint.

He's an artist.

Mom said he's a good artist.

Dad comes to see Sam and me
on Saturdays.

Sometimes we go to the park to
play ball.

This is Jane.

Jane cares for us when Mom
is at work.
She comes every day.

Every day the first thing Jane
does is get into her blue dress.
We keep it here.
It's a nice dress.

Then she makes something for us
to eat.

"Well, what to make?"
she will say.

"Mushy eggs," we say.

"Mushy eggs, mushy eggs,"
she will say.
"O.K., O.K., mushy eggs."

Mushy eggs are like scrambled
eggs, only mushy.
Jane makes good mushy eggs.

Then Jane makes us do the work
we do for money.

When we have rain, we must stay
in.

Then Jane will play with us.

Jane will let us ride on her back.

Sometimes we'll sing and dance.

I'll play my drum.

Sam will dance.

And Jane will sing songs about
Spain.

We have a lot of laughs.

Sometimes Jane will tell us about
Spain and when she was a little girl.

That was the way things were—
until a little while back.

Then one day Jane told us she
would go back to Spain.

"It's nice in Spain," she said.
"And I want to be with my
old friends.
I didn't want to leave them."

Mom took us to the boat the day
Jane went away.

We didn't want to say good-by
to each other.

But we had to.

Then we went home.

I went to my room to be alone
for a while.

I didn't feel good.

I began to think that nothing
would be good again.

Sam was mad!

At Jane, I think.

He said over and over, "I don't
like that Jane that went away!"

But then he looked at her dress
and he began to feel bad.

Mom had to stay home with us

for a while after Jane went away.

We had fun.

Now we have a new person that
cares for us.

This is Molly.

She is nice.

Maybe I'll love Molly, too.

Molly makes good scrambled eggs.

But she doesn't know how to
make mushy eggs.

I'm Not Oscar's Friend

We work with words.

across   alone   ahead

regular   mayor   weather

Sound the words.

ago

Oscar

forever

months

score

she'll

doctor

Sight words.

That <u>sure</u> won't help Oscar.

They aren't <u>your</u> friends.

<u>Who</u> are your <u>enemies</u>?

There is this boy, Oscar, who is
down the street.

One time I was his friend.

But a few days ago he said
something mean to me.

So mean I won't tell you what it
was.

So I said something mean back.

And he said something more mean
to me.

And then we were not friends.

It only took a little while to make enemies with Oscar.

But it will take forever to make up.

Forever is like never.

You see, I'll never make up with Oscar.

When we were friends, there was a
game we used to play.

After three months my score was 265.

Oscar's score was only 73.

And now Oscar has lost his chance to
catch up in the game.

Oscar's score will be 73 forever.

What is so good about Oscar?

He used to call at dinner time!

And I would be nice and talk to him.

Have you ever had cold hot food?

I'm sure Oscar would like to see me.

He'll want to play with me.

But then he'll think about the

mean things he said to me.

And he'll know that we aren't

friends.

Oscar will put on one red sock and
one brown sock.

You see, he'll think about me
and not the red sock and brown sock.

Then he'll see that his
shirt is inside out.

He'll want to know how that came
to be.

When someone comes to the door,
Oscar will think it's me.

He'll run to open it.

But it will only be the
person who comes to clean.

Oscar will tell her his trouble.

She'll let him help her clean.

The house will get clean.

But that sure won't help Oscar.

She'll tell him that soon
he and I will be all made up.

But that's not true.

You see, I'll never make up with you, Oscar.

I'll be one of your enemies forever.

Months and months and months will go by.

And I still won't be your friend.

Maybe your mother will think you are sick.

She'll take you to the doctor.

And that sure won't be any fun.

The doctor will tell you that you are well.

But she'll make you get your shots.

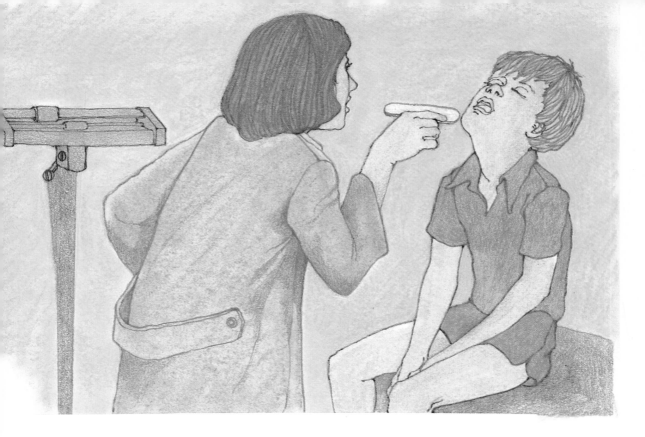

You didn't know how good things
were, Oscar.

I feel sorry for you.

I sure do feel sorry for Oscar.

I feel so sorry for him that I'll
let him make up with me.

I'll walk by his house.

If he's out, I'll let him make
up with me.

Here I come, Oscar.

So where are you?

This was your big chance to get

me back.

But you let it go by.

Well, I could go up to your door.

No, you could begin to think that

I wanted to make up with you.

Well, you will never have a chance

to be my friend.

You will have to play with Alfred,

and I know you can't stand him.

Or Jill, if you can put up with her.

Your brother is around, but he is

only three.

Boy, do I feel sorry for you, Oscar.

Maybe I should give Oscar one more chance.

I could call him.

Hello, Oscar.

I'll let you be my friend.

What?

Don't you remember?

A few days ago.

Sure, a big one.

Oh, well.

Why don't you come over and see
my new truck?

O.K.

Good-by.

Oscar can't remember things too well.

What would he do if he didn't have
me for a friend?

Myrtle the Turtle and the Party

We work with words.

stopped	funny	hotter
sadly	likely	slowly
find	mind	child

Sound the words.

plodded

lonely

kind

rabbit

gift

behind

party

squirrel

surprise

Sight words.

<u>Myrtle</u> watched <u>Ruthie</u> Rabbit go away.

Myrtle the Turtle plodded down
the road.

She looked this way.

She looked that way.

She saw no one.

Deep inside it made her lonely.

It was a good day to talk to
someone, but there was no one around.

Then Myrtle the Turtle saw Ruthie
Rabbit come down the road.

"Good," Myrtle said, "here is
someone I can talk with."

But Ruthie Rabbit just said, "Hello,
Myrtle," and went on by her.

Myrtle watched Ruthie Rabbit go
away.

Ruthie had a gift behind her back.

"Oh!" said Myrtle.

"She is on her way to a party.

That's why she didn't stop."

Myrtle plodded on down the road.

Soon she saw Sam Squirrel come down
the road.

"Good," said Myrtle, "now I have
someone to talk with."

But Sam Squirrel just said, "Hello,
Myrtle," and went on by her.

Myrtle watched Sam Squirrel as he
went away.

He had a gift behind his back, too.

"He's going to a party, too," said
Myrtle.

"That's why he didn't stop."

Just then Fred Frog came up the
road.

"Good," said Myrtle, "here is
someone to talk with.
Fred Frog never goes to a party."

But Fred Frog just said, "Good
day," and he, too, went on by.

Myrtle looked.
He had a gift behind his back, too.

"Well, now," said Myrtle, "he is
going to a party, too.

Everyone is going to a party today—
everyone but me."

She began to think some more.
"If all my friends are going to a
party, it must be for someone I know.
But no one wanted me to come."

That made Myrtle feel lonely.
She plodded back home.

She began to think.

"It would be nice to have someone
over for tea.

But no one is home.

No one but me, that is.

Oh, well.

I will just have to have tea alone.

I will have some cake, too."

Myrtle went inside.

Then she heard, "Surprise! Surprise!

Happy birthday, Myrtle."

There were all her friends.

Each one had a gift for Myrtle.

The party all her friends were
going to was for her.

They all had cake and tea.

Myrtle said, "Oh, what good, kind
friends!

I have never had this kind of
surprise before."

But Myrtle never did tell her
friends her surprise for them.

Her birthday was still two
months away.

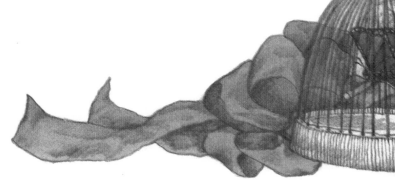

New Places,
New Faces

The Gingerbread Man

We work with words.

above   color   wonder

mixture   creature   nature

most   roll   poll

Sound the words.

oven

done

pasture

rolled

Sight words.

The gingerbread man laughed at the woman.

Soon he was gone.

One time there was a little
old woman and a little old man.

They lived all alone in a little
old house.

They didn't have any children.
So one day the little old woman
made a little gingerbread man.

She rolled him out.

Then she put him in a pan to cook.

She put the pan in the oven and shut
the oven door.

"When he's done I'll have a little
gingerbread man," she said.

Soon the gingerbread man was done.

The little old woman took him out of
the oven.

The gingerbread man rolled out of the pan.

"Now that I am done," he said, "I will run away."

He rolled out the door, down the street, and away.

The little old woman and the little old man ran after him.

They ran as fast as they could.

"Run, run as fast as you can!
You can't catch me.
I'm the gingerbread man!" he said.

And they could not catch him.

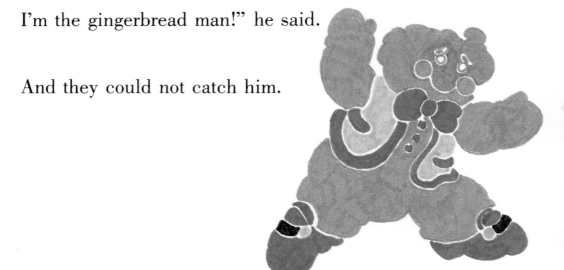

The gingerbread man ran on and on.

He came to a cow by the road.

"Stop, gingerbread man," said the
cow.

"I want to eat you."

But the gingerbread man just laughed.

He said, "I have run away from a
little old woman and a little old man.

And I can run away from you, I can!"

And as the cow ran after him, he
looked back.

He said, "Run, run as fast as you can.

You can't catch me.

I'm the gingerbread man!"

And the cow could not catch him.

The gingerbread man ran on until
he came to a horse in a pasture.

"Stop, gingerbread man," said the
horse.

"You look good to eat."

But the gingerbread man laughed.

He said, "I have run away from a
little old woman.

I have run away from a little old
man and a cow.

And I can run away from you, I can!"

And the horse ran after him.

The gingerbread man looked back
and said, "Run, run as fast as you can!

You can't catch me.

I'm the gingerbread man!"

And the horse could not catch him.

By and by the gingerbread man came
to some people.

They tried to pick him up.

When he didn't stop, they said,
"Don't run so fast.

You look good to eat."

But the gingerbread man ran faster
still.

He ran down to a pasture.

As he ran he looked back and said,
"I have run away from an old woman,
an old man, a cow, and a horse.

And I can run away from you, I can!"

Then he laughed and said, "Run, run,
as fast as you can!

You can't catch me.

I'm the gingerbread man!"

And the people could not catch him.

Soon he saw a fox in the pasture.

The fox looked at the gingerbread
man and began to run.

"You can't catch me," the gingerbread
man said to the fox.

"Well, I would not catch you if I
could," said the fox.

"I don't like gingerbread."

Just then the gingerbread man came
to a lake in the pasture.

He could not swim across it.

He didn't want to get wet.

But he wanted to keep away from

the cow, the horse, and the people.

"Jump on my tail, and I will take you across," said the fox.

The gingerbread man got on his tail.
The fox went into the lake.
After a little while he said,
"I would not want to get you wet.
Jump on my back."

They were just about across.
The fox said, "Oh, my.
This water is too deep.
I would not want you to get wet.
Jump on my nose."

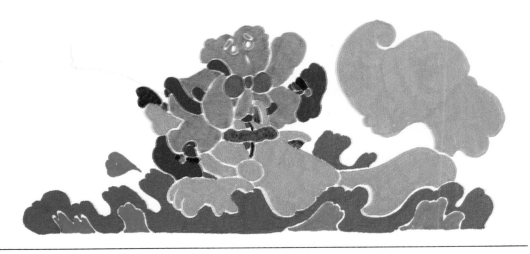

So the gingerbread man got up on
his nose.

Soon they were across the lake.
And the fox took a big bite out of
the gingerbread man.

"Oh, my!" said the gingerbread man.
"A big bite of me is gone."

In a little while the gingerbread
man said, "Oh, my!
One more big bite of me is gone."

And after that, the gingerbread
man never said one thing.
He was all gone.

Gingerbread for Everyone

We work with words.

garden   target   starch

drawing   laughing   whispering

Sound the words.

start

bowl

mixing

stir

Sight words.

<u>Together</u> we can roll out the <u>dough</u>.

I like to eat good things.

And I like water.

Fruit, cheese, and bread with
jam are good, too.

But just between you and me,
I love gingerbread best of all.

When it just comes out of the oven,
I like it even better.

The best part is that I can make gingerbread.

You can, too!

I'll show you how.

Let's start.

You will have to get these things ready.

This will go in one bowl.

You will mix these up in the other bowl.

You need to start your oven.

That way, it will get hot.

Now you can make the gingerbread dough.

Mix all these things together.

Then you get dough.

Start by mixing these things in one mixing bowl.

Stir and stir.

Mix it all together.

Get out your other mixing bowl.

Put the other things in it.

Now stir all this together.

The next part is a lot of fun.

You put this on your hands.

Then you mix what is in each
bowl together.

Do it with your hands.

The dough is so mushy!

You need to roll it and roll it.
Roll it out hard!

Then you can make a gingerbread boy
or girl.
You can even make a gingerbread tree
or cat.
Did you ever eat a gingerbread cow?
Put your gingerbread in to cook.
Soon will come the best part of all.
You can eat gingerbread!

Why the Jackal Won't Talk to the Hedgehog —

We work with words.

bridge	ledge	page
total	numeral	formal

Sound the words.

hedgehog

jackal

stalks

angry

Sight words.

They went to the field to get some onions.

The onions were very good to eat.

One time there was a small
farm.

There the jackal lived.

His friend, the hedgehog, lived there, too.

Each day they went out to work.

They went to work in their wheat field.

They took away the plants that would
hurt their wheat.

And they picked up all of the
loose rocks.

And they took them away.

Soon their field was very clean.

They planted the wheat.

Soon the wheat was ripe.

It was time to harvest.

The hedgehog said, "You must take some
of the harvest.

And I must take some of it.

You pick first.

Do you want what is in the ground?

Or do you want what is on top?"

Now, the jackal didn't think too well.

"I'll want what is in the ground,"
he said.

So the jackal got the parts he
could not eat.

But the hedgehog got all the good
parts.

And he could eat them.

The jackal didn't feel well.

He was very angry.

He didn't like what the hedgehog
did to him.

He had cup after cup of water.

"Now I feel better," he said.

"I must not do that the next time."

Soon they had to plant onions.

The jackal went out to the field.

The hedgehog went with him.

They got the field ready.

Then they planted the onions.

The stalks of the onions got bigger
and bigger each day.

And each day got more and more hot.

Soon the onions were ripe.

The stalks fell over on the ground.

The hedgehog went
back to the field.

The jackal went with him.

The hedgehog said to the jackal, "It's
time to harvest.

You take your part first."

"Not this time," said the jackal.

"I won't fall for your tricks.

I'll take what is on top of the ground."

The jackal was not angry.

He was happy.

He cut all the stalks.

Then he saw the hedgehog take all the

onions.

Now the jackal was very angry.

He went away from the farm.

And that is why, to even this day, the
jackal won't talk to the hedgehog.

Little Una _____

We work with words.

become   below   beside

shipment   enjoyment   refreshment

Sound the words.

because

announcement

called

Una

mayor

council

banner

Sight word.

Little Una was a <u>rhinoceros</u>.

In a place a long way away
there is a city.

In the city there is a park.
In the park there is a zoo.
And in the zoo there is a rhinoceros.
She is called Little Una.

This is her story.

Little Una looked ugly.
She had a big ugly face.
Her hide looked ugly, too.
It looked like a pile of rocks.

But Little Una was nice.

She had a lot of friends.

All the children loved her.

Children always came to see her.

And they would always have food for her.

Little Una could eat all of it.

Because you see, she was very big.

Of all the animals in the zoo, people
liked Little Una the best.

One day the mayor called
the city council together.

Then he made an announcement.

"I think," said the mayor, "that
we will put a stone in the park.

We could put a picture of each one
of us on the stone."

The council was happy about the
announcement.

They all wanted their pictures on
the stone.

"But to put up a stone," said
the mayor, "we need money.

We will need to sell the rhinoceros."

The children heard about the
stone.

They all went to the park.

"I don't want a stone!" said
one boy.

"I want Little Una," said his sister.

All the children began to cry because
they loved Little Una.

"Let's stop the mayor.
He can't sell Little Una," the
children all said.

The very next day, people looked up into the air.

In the air, they could see a big banner.

"VOTE FOR LITTLE UNA FOR MAYOR," it read.

Everyone saw the banner.

"Let's vote for her," said one father.

"Let's do!" said a person.
"That will show the mayor.
He can't sell Little Una!"

The mayor and his council looked up.
They, too, saw the banner in the air.
The mayor smiled.
His council laughed.

But the people went to work.
Soon, more than one banner was up.

And all were for Little Una.

There was even a picture of Little
Una in the paper.

Everyone said, "Vote for Little Una!"

On one day everyone came to vote.
Soon it was all over.
Little Una and the children had won!

The mayor called his council together.

"I have an announcement to make,"

he said.

"The children have won.

We must not put up a stone.

We can't sell the rhinoceros."

Now everyone was happy.

The children laughed.

Everyone sang.

There was a big party.

It went long into the night.

But the best part was that Little

Una could stay!

ACKNOWLEDGMENTS

Grateful acknowledgment is given for permission to reprint the following copyrighted material:

"Alfred Snood" adaptation by permission of G. P. Putnam's Sons from *Alfred Snood* by Joan Hanson. Copyright © 1972 by Joan Hanson.

"The Gingerbread Man" from *Stories to Tell to Children* by Sara Cone Bryant. Copyright 1907, 1935. Reprinted by permission of Houghton Mifflin Company.

"Going to Bed" from *Around and About* by Marchette Chute. Copyright 1957 (E. P. Dutton) and reprinted by permission of the author.

"He's My Brother" adapted from *He's My Brother* © 1974 by Joe Lasker. Reprinted with permission of Albert Whitman & Company.

"I'm Not Oscar's Friend" from *I'm Not Oscar's Friend Anymore* by Marjorie Weinman Sharmat. Copyright © 1975 by Marjorie Weinman Sharmat. Reprinted by permission of the publishers, E. P. Dutton.

"The King's Wish" adapted from *The King's Wish and Other Stories* by Benjamin Elkin, by permission of Random House, Inc. Copyright © 1960 by Benjamin Elkin.

"Leave Herbert Alone" adapted from *Leave Herbert Alone*, © 1972, by Alma Marshak Whitney, by permission of Addison-Wesley Publishing Company, Inc.

"Little Una" adapted from *Little Una* by Elizabeth Olds with the permission of Charles Scribner's Sons, copyright © 1963 Elizabeth Olds.

"Max" reprinted with permission of Macmillan Publishing Company, Inc., from *Max* by Rachel Isadora. Copyright © 1976 by Rachel Isadora.

"Mr. Spats" by Shel Silverstein. Copyright Shel Silverstein, 1966. Used by permission.

"Mushy Eggs" adaptation by permission of G. P. Putnam's Sons and Raines and Raines from *Mushy Eggs* by Florence Adams. Copyright © 1973 by Florence Adams.

"Myrtle the Turtle and the Party" reprinted from *Instructor* copyright © June 1962 by the Instructor Publications, Inc., used by permission.

"Natsook" adapted from *The Golden Magazine* (now *Young World*), copyright © 1970 by Review Publishing Company, Inc., Indianapolis, Indiana.

"The New System" adapted from *Jack and Jill* magazine, copyright © 1977 by The Saturday Evening Post Company, Indianapolis, Indiana.

"No Cows Where Morris Lived" adapted from *Children's Playmate Magazine*, copyright © 1971 by Review Publishing Company, Inc., Indianapolis, Indiana.

"Oh No, Cat!" adaptation by permission of Coward, McCann and Geoghegan, Inc., from *Oh No, Cat!* by Janice May Udry. Copyright © 1976 by Janice May Udry.

"Squash Pie" abridgment and adaptation of *Squash Pie* by Wilson Gage (without illustrations). Copyright text © 1976 by Wilson Gage. By permission of Greenwillow Books (A Division of William Morrow & Company).

"Why the Jackal Won't Talk to the Hedgehog" adapted from *Why the Jackal Won't Speak to the Hedgehog* by Harold Berson. Copyright © 1969 by Harold Berson. Used by permission of The Seabury Press.

Grateful acknowledgment is made to the following for illustrations and photographs on the pages indicated:

Ellen Blonder 7-10; Mike Durbin 103-116; Linda Edwards 175-185; Elizabeth Fong 11-24, 215-222; Susan Gilmour 43-62; Maryanne Regal Hoburg 77-84; Pat Hoggan 146, 147, 187-200; Connie Hwang 148-160; Rachel Isadora 129-137, Mary Knowles 63-75; Pat Maloney 85-90, 101; Diane McElwain 91-100; Murray McKeehan 117-128, 207-214; Gale Turner 25-41; Connie Warton 139-145; Peg Zych 161-174, 201-206.

2 3 4 5 6 7 8 9 10 D 87 86 85 84 83 82 81 80